With Open Hands

WITH OPEN HANDS

TEXT BY
Henri J.M. Nouwen

PHOTOGRAPHY BY
Ron P. van den Bosch
and
Theo Robert

AVE MARIA PRESS • NOTRE DAME, INDIANA 46556

Eighth printing, October 1975
Over 115,000 in print

Library of Congress Catalog Card Number: 71-177600
ISBN: 0-87793-040-6

Translated from an original manuscript in Dutch,
Met Open Handen, by Patrick Gaffney

Photo Credits:
Theo Robert: 11, 18, 19, 27, 29, 35, 45, 53, 54, 61, 67, 68, 75, 77, 83,
        91, 93, 99, 111, 113, 119, 121, 127, 130, 131, 133, 153,
        155, 159, 160
Ron P. van den Bosch: 13, 15, 21, 23, 30, 31, 34, 37, 39, 42, 43, 47, 49,
        55, 58, 59, 63, 65, 71, 79, 87, 96, 97, 101, 103, 105, 107,
        108, 109, 110, 124, 125, 136, 137, 140, 141, 143, 149, 156
Wim Nouwen: 106, 115, 145

Layout by *Doris Kohl*

Printed in the United States of America

CONTENTS

Foreword

The ideas gathered together in this book were slow in coming. It all began with my attempt to speak personally about a number of experiences with praying. For I thought I could hardly write about prayer before I had asked the question: "What is it that I myself find in prayer?" I came to see that praying had something to do with silence, with acceptance, with hope, with compassion, and even with revolution. Then I carefully sought out concepts and images which expressed what I had experienced or would have liked to experience.

But what does this have to do with anyone else? Aren't my own experiences so personal that they might just as well remain hidden? Or could it be that what is most personal for me, what rings true to the depths of my being, also has meaning for others? Ultimately, I believe that what is most personal is also the most universal. To arrive at this point, however, friends are necessary, for they are the ones who help you distinguish between superficial sensations and deep human experiences.

This conviction led me to invite twenty-five theology students to form a group which would begin with my first hesitant formulations and help work out a better understanding of what praying really involves. During the seven meetings which followed, there was very little discussion or argument; what did result were living experiences, in the course of which the illusive phenomenon we call prayer became an ever more tangible reality.

The text which resulted is not the work of a single author; it was distilled from numerous contributions. It took form during many hours of intimate conversation which could possibly be called hours of praying.

But words are only one way to express the reality of prayer. Maybe our eyes are more sympathetic to photo-images with the many shades of dark and light, than to the black words printed on white paper. So two friends, Ron van den Bosch and Theo Robert, tried to look at life through the eye of a contemplative camera and to rediscover the moments of prayer in the faces of man and the forms of the world in which he lives. And just as the students searched in their own lives for those precious moments of prayer, so Ron and Theo went through the cities, the villages and the countrysides to see the living witnesses of man's attempt to stretch beyond the boundaries of his own limitation.

I hope the words and photo-images brought together here are more than the expression of the experiences and aspirations of a small group of students and photographers. They are presented as "reflections" of life in which many, hopefully, will be able to recognize themselves. I wish to express special thanks to Patrick Gaffney, not only for his careful translation of the Dutch manuscript, but also for his faithful friendship during the year in which this book was made; to my brother Wim who generously offered some of the photographs he made during his hitchhike travels in the United States to be used by Ron and Theo; and to Doris Kohl who helped all of us by her encouragement, her original ideas, and her skillful work on the layout.

Henri J. M. Nouwen
Utrecht

With Clenched Fists

PRAYING is no easy matter. It demands a relationship in which you allow the other to enter into the very center of your person, allow him to speak there, allow him to touch the sensitive core of your being, and allow him to see so much that you would rather leave in darkness. And when do you really want to do that? Perhaps you would let the other come across the threshold to say something, to touch something, but to let him into that place where your life gets its form, that is dangerous and calls for defense.

The resistance to praying is like the resistance of tightly clenched fists. This image shows the tension, the desire to cling tightly to yourself, a greediness which betrays fear. The story about an old woman brought to a psychiatric center exemplifies this attitude. She was wild, swinging at everything in sight, and scaring everyone so much that the doctors had to take everything away from her. But there was one small coin which she gripped in her fist and would not give up. In fact, it took two men to pry open that squeezed hand. It was as though she would lose her very self along with the coin. If they deprived her of that last possession, she would have nothing more, and be nothing more. That was her fear.

The man invited to pray is asked to open his tightly clenched fists and to give up his last coin. But who wants to do that? A first prayer, therefore, is often a painful prayer, because you discover you don't want to let go. You hold fast to what is familiar, even if you aren't proud of it. You find yourself saying: "That's just how it is with me. I would like it to be different, but it can't be now. That's just the way it is, and that's the way I'll have to leave it." Once you talk like that you've already given up the belief that your life might be otherwise, you've already let the hope for a new life float by. Since you wouldn't dare to put a question mark behind a bit of your own experience with all its attachments, you have wrapped yourself up in the destiny of facts. You feel it is safer to cling to a sorry past than to trust in a new future. So you fill your hands with small clammy coins which you don't want to surrender.

You still feel bitter because that girl wasn't grateful for something you gave her; you still feel jealous of the fellow who is better paid than you are, you still want revenge on someone who doesn't respect you, you are still disappointed that you've received no letter, still angry because she didn't smile when you walked by. You live through it, you live along with it as though it didn't really bother you . . . until the moment that you want to pray. Then everything returns: the bitterness, the hate, the jealousy, the disappointment and the desire for revenge. But these feelings are not just there, you clutch them in your hands as if they were treasures you didn't want to part with. You sit rummaging in all that old sourness as if you couldn't do without it, as if in giving it up, you would lose your very self.

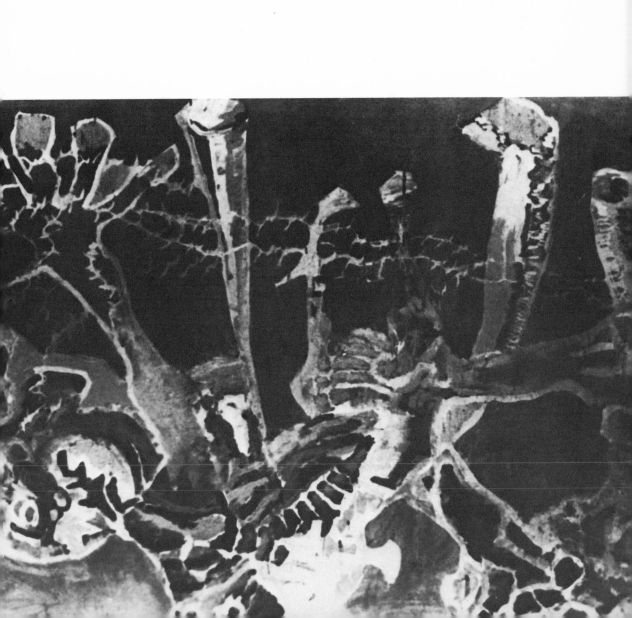

Detachment is often understood as letting loose of what is attractive. But it can also mean being attached to what is repulsive. You can become attached to your own hate. As long as you look for retaliation, you are riveted to your own past. Sometimes it appears as though you would lose yourself along with your revenge and hate — so you stand there with balled-up fists, closed to the other who wants to heal.

When you want to pray, then, the first question is: How do I open my closed hands? Certainly not by violence. Nor by a compulsive decision. Perhaps you can find a way to prayer in the words of the angel to the frightened shepherds, the same words the risen Lord spoke to his disciples: "Don't be afraid." Don't be afraid of him who wants to enter that space where you live, or to let him see what you are clinging to so anxiously. Don't be afraid to show the clammy coin which will buy so little anyway. Don't be afraid to offer your hate, bitterness, disappointment to him who reveals himself as love. Even if you know you have little to show, don't be afraid to let it be seen. You keep catching yourself wanting to deceive the other by putting on a semblance of beauty, by holding back everything dirty and spoiled, by clearing a little path that looks very proper. But that is compulsive, forced and artificial; it exhausts you and turns prayer into torment.

When you dare to let go and surrender one of those many fears, your hand relaxes and your palms spread out in a gesture of receiving. You must have patience, of course, before your hands are completely open and their muscles relaxed.

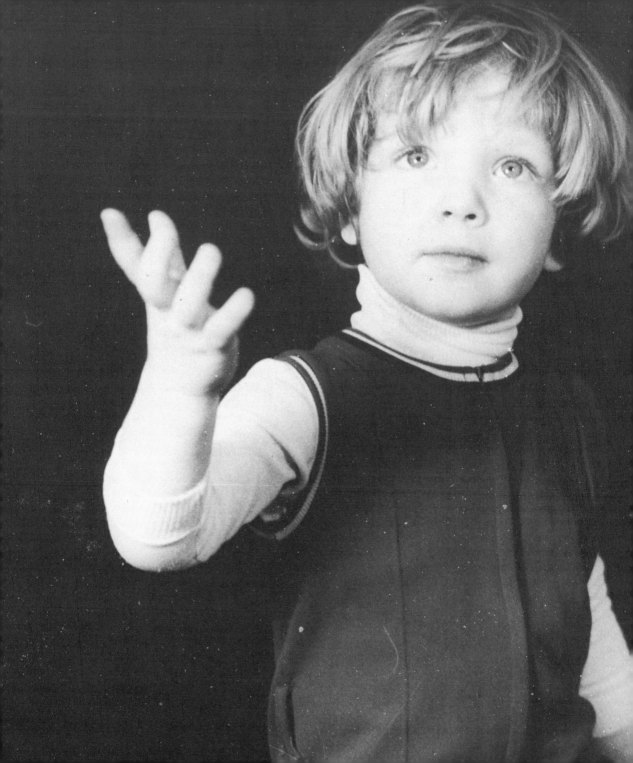

You can never fully achieve such an attitude, for behind each fist another one is hiding, and sometimes the process seems endless. Much has happened in your life to make all these fists. . . . At any hour of the day or night you might clench again for fear.

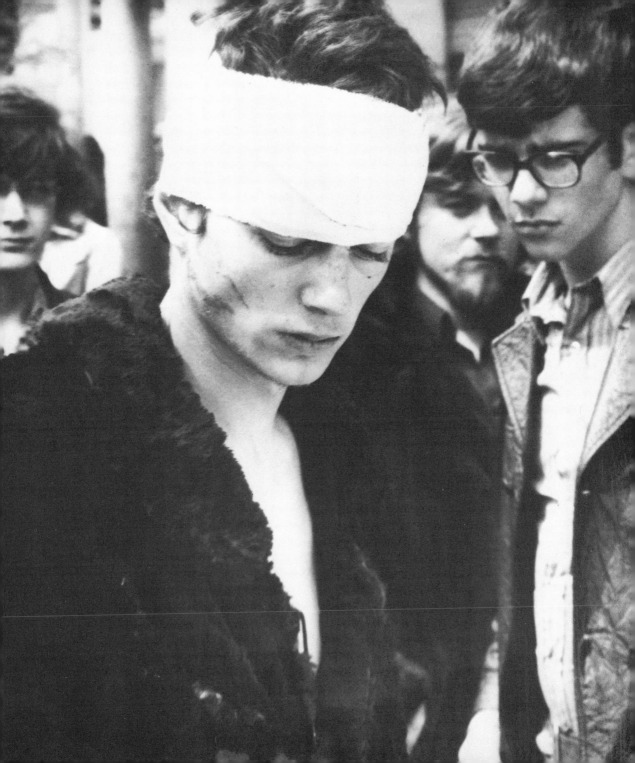

Someone will tell you, "You have to be able to forgive yourself." But that isn't possible. What is possible is to open your hands without fear, so the other can blow your sins away. For perhaps it isn't clammy coins, but just a light dust which a soft breeze will whirl away, leaving only a grin or a chuckle behind. Then you feel a bit of new freedom, and praying becomes a joy, a spontaneous reaction to the world and the people around you. Praying becomes effortless, inspired and lively, or peaceful and quiet. Then you recognize the festive and the modest as moments of prayer. You begin to suspect that to pray is to live.

CHAPTER 1

Prayer and Silence

WE know there is some connection between prayer and silence, but if we think about silence in our life it seems that it isn't always peaceful; silence can also be frightening.

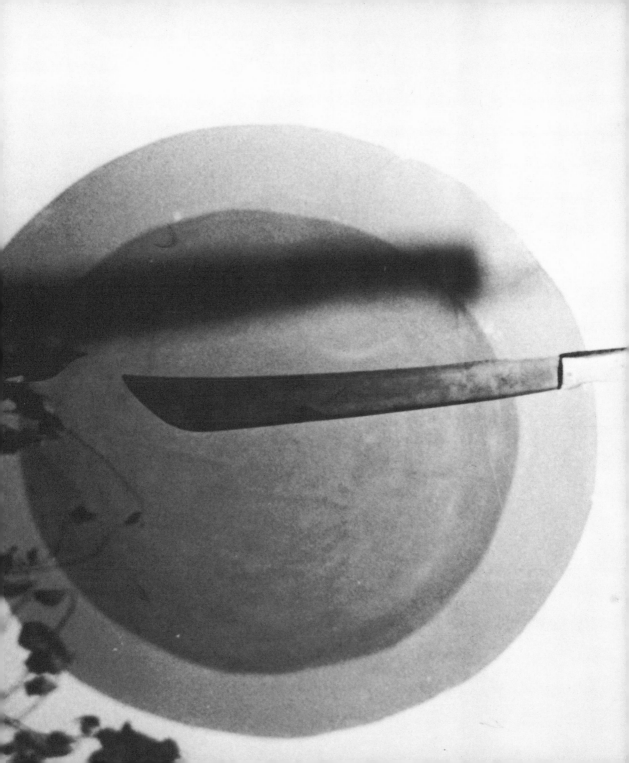

One student who had thought deeply about the silence in his life wrote:

Silence is night
and just as there are nights
with no moon and no stars
when you're all alone
totally alone
when you're cursed
when you become a nothing
which no one needs —
so there are silences
which are threatening
because there is nothing except
the silence
there can be nothing except
the silence.
Even if you open your ears
and your eyes
it keeps going on
without hope or relief.
Night with no light, no hope
I am alone
in my guilt
without forgiveness
without love.
Then, desperately, I go looking
for friends
then I walk the streets
a body
a sign
a sound
for nothing.

But there are also nights
with stars
with a full moon
with the light from a house
in the distance
and silences which are peaceful
and reflective
the noise of a sparrow
in a large empty church
when my heart wants to sing out
with joy
when I feel that I'm not alone
when I'm expecting
friends
or remember
a couple words
from a poem I read lately
when I lose myself in a
Hail Mary
or the somber voice of a psalm
when I am me
and you are you
when we aren't afraid of
each other
when we leave all talk to
the angel
who brought us the silence
and peace.

Just as there are two nights, there are two silences, one is frightening and the other is peaceful. For many, silence is threatening. They don't know what to do with it. If they leave the noise of the city behind and come upon a place where no cars are roaring, no ships are tooting, no trains rumbling, where there is no hum of radio or television, where no records or tapes are playing, they feel their entire body gripped by an intense unrest. They feel like a fish which has been set on dry land. They have lost their bearings. There are some students who can't study without a solid wall of music surrounding them. If they are forced to sit in a room without that constant flow of sound, they grow very nervous.

Thus, for many of us, silence has become a real disturbance. There was a time when silence was normal and a lot of racket disturbed us. But today, noise is the normal fare, and silence, strange as it may seem, has become the real disturbance. It is not hard to understand, therefore, that people who experience silence in this way will have difficulty with prayer.

We have become alienated from silence. If we go to the beach, or on a picnic in the woods, the transistor radio is often our most important companion. Perhaps we should say that we can't stand the sound of silence.

Silence is full of noise. The wind murmuring, the leaves rustling, the birds flapping their wings, the waves washing ashore. And even if these noises cannot be heard, there is still the breathing of a quiet man, the motion of his hand over his skin, the swallowing of his throat, and the soft patter of footfalls. But we have become deaf to this thundering silence. It seems that it can't be heard anymore without the help of amplifiers.

If a person is invited to exchange this noise for silence, it is often a frightening proposal. He feels like a child who sees the walls of a house collapse and suddenly finds himself in an open field, or like a woman who is violently stripped of her clothing, or like a bird torn away from its nest. His ears begin to ache because the familiar sounds are missing and his body needs that noise as a downy blanket which kept it warm. The man who is thus sent into silence is like the dope addict who must go through the painful withdrawal process.

But still more difficult than getting rid of that surrounding din is the achievement of inner silence, a silence of the heart which goes beyond every man. It seems that a person who is caught up in all that noise has lost touch with his own inner self. The questions which are asked from within go unanswered. The unsure feelings are not cleared up and the tangled desires are not straightened out, the confusing emotions are not understood. All that remains is a chaotic tumble of feelings which have never had a chance to be cured because the man constantly let himself be distracted by a world demanding all his attention.

It is hardly a surprise, therefore, that when all the daily racket is shut off, a new noise turns on, rising out of all those vague feelings which scream for attention. The person who enters a quiet room still doesn't experience inner silence. When there is no one to talk to, and no one to listen to, an interior discussion starts up which almost seems to get out of hand. The many unsolved problems demand attention, one care forces itself upon the other, one complaint rivals the next, all plead for a hearing. Sometimes a person is left powerless in the face of twisted sentiments which he cannot untangle.

It makes you wonder if the diversion we look for in the many things outside us might not be an attempt to avoid a confrontation with what is inside. "What should I begin when I'm through with all my work?" This question leads many people to flee from themselves and to hold fast to any number of things which make them feel like they're still busy. It's as if they were saying: "Where do I turn when I have no more friends to talk with, no music to listen to, no paper to read, and no films to see?" The problem here is not whether a person can live without friends or without feeding his eyes and ears, but that there are many people who can't stand to be alone, to shut their eyes, to gently push aside all the assorted noises and to sit calmly and quietly.

To be calm and quiet all by yourself is hardly the same as sleeping. In fact, it means being fully awake and following with close attention every move going on inside you. It involves a self-discipline where the urge to get up and go is recognized as a temptation to look elsewhere for what is really close at hand. It is the freedom to stroll in your own yard, to rake up the leaves and clear the paths so you can easily find your way. Perhaps there will be much fear and uncertainty when we first come upon this "unfamiliar terrain," but slowly and surely we begin to see developing an order and a familiarity which summon our longing to stay home.

With this new confidence, we recapture our own life afresh, from within. Along with the new knowledge of our "inner space" where feelings of love and hate, tenderness and pain, forgiveness and greed are separated, strengthened or reformed, there emerges the mastery of the gentle hand. This is the hand of the gardener who carefully makes space for a new plant to grow, and who doesn't pull weeds too rashly, but only uproots those which threaten to choke the young life. Under his gentle regime, a man once again becomes master over his own house. Not only over his day, but over his night as well. Not only when he is awake, but also when he sleeps. For he who has the day, will gain the night as well. Sleep is no longer a strange darkness, but a friendly curtain behind which dreams continue to live and to send out messages which can be gratefully received. The paths of his dreams are as trusty as the paths of his waking hours and there is no longer any need to be afraid.

If we do not shun silence, all this is possible. But it is not easy. Noise from the outside keeps demanding our attention, and restlessness from within keeps stirring up our anxiety. Many people feel trapped between this temptation and this fear. Since they can't turn inward, they look for calm in the noises, even when they know they will never find it there.

But whenever you do come upon this silence, it seems as though you have received a gift, one which is "promising" in the true sense of the word. The promise of this silence is that new life can be born. It is this silence which is the silence of peace and prayer, because you are brought back to the other who is leading you. In this silence you lose the feeling of being compulsive and you find yourself a person who can be himself along with other things and other people.

Then you realize that you can do many things, but it isn't necessary. It is the silence of the "poor in spirit," where you learn to see your life in its proper perspectives. In this silence, the false pretenses fade away and you can see the world again with a certain distance, and in the midst of all your cares, you can pray with the psalmist:

> If Yahweh does not build the house,
>   in vain the masons toil;
> if Yahweh does not guard the city,
>   in vain the sentries watch.
>   (Psalm 127)

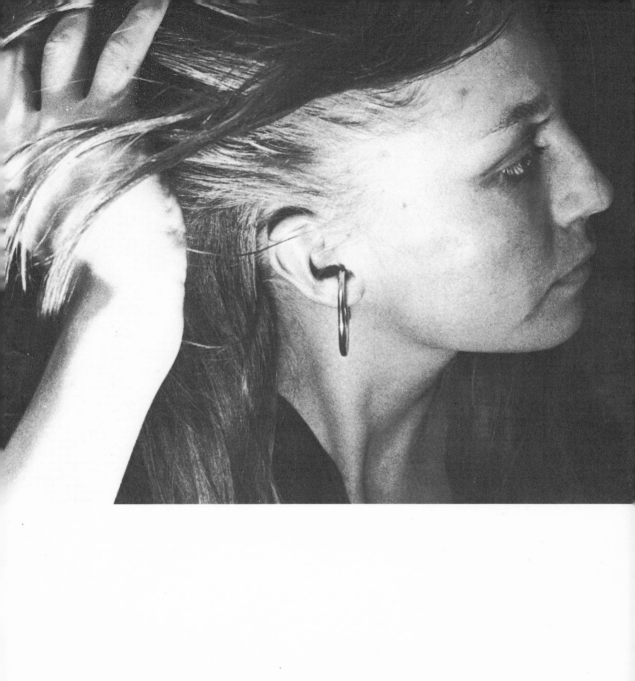

CHAPTER 2

Prayer and Acceptance

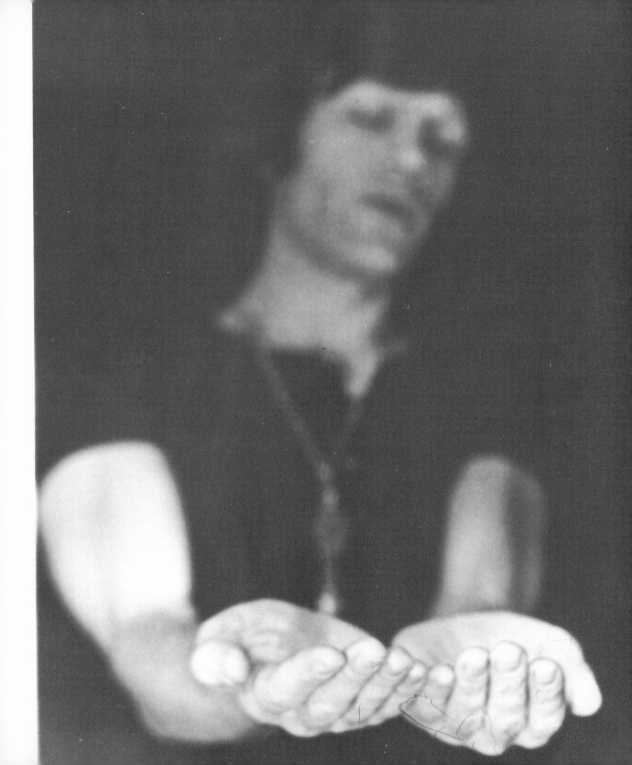

DEEP silence leads us to suspect that, in the first place, prayer is acceptance. A man who prays is a man standing with his hands open to the world. He knows that God will show himself in the nature which surrounds him, in the people he meets, in the situations he runs into. He trusts that the world holds God's secret within it, and he expects that secret to be shown to him. Prayer creates that openness where God can give himself to man. Indeed, God wants to give himself; he wants to surrender himself to the man he has created, he even begs to be admitted into the human heart.

This openness, however, does not simply come of itself. It requires our confession that we are limited, dependent, weak and even sinful. Whenever you pray, you profess that you are not God and that you wouldn't want to be, that you haven't reached your goal yet, and that you never will reach it in this life, that you must constantly stretch out your hands and wait again for the gift which gives new life. This attitude is difficult because it makes you vulnerable.

The wisdom of the world is the wisdom which says: "It is best to stand firm, to get a good grip on what's yours here and now, and hold your own against the rest who want to take it away from you; you've got to be on your guard against ambush. If you don't carry a weapon, if you don't make a fist, and don't scramble to get what little you need — food and shelter — then you're just asking to be threadbare and destitute, and you'll end up trying to find a mediocre satisfaction in a generosity which no one understands. You open your hands and they pound in nails! A smart man doesn't look for anything too far away. He keeps on his toes, with his muscles tense, his fists clenched; he squints and is always ready for an unexpected attack."

That's what a person's inner life often looks like. If you nurture thoughts of peace, you have to be open and receiving. But can you do it, do you dare? Suspicion, jealousy, hate, revenge, resentment and greed are there before you've even given them a name. "What's he really trying to do?" "What's actually on his mind?" "He must not be laying all the cards on the table." "There's certainly more to his remark than meets the eye." Often such feelings arise even before thoughts can be formulated. Something deep inside has already tightened up: "Watch out, plan your tactic and hold your weapons in position." Then thoughts of peace are far away. You fear they are too dangerous or impractical. You think: "Anyone who doesn't arm himself shares the guilt for his own fall."

How can you expect a gift in this mood? Can you even imagine that your life could be any other way? It's no wonder that praying presents such a problem, for it requires a constant readiness to lay the weapons down and to let go of your feelings which tell you to keep the things around you at a distance. Instead you live in constant expectation that God who makes everything new will cause you to be born again.

A person becomes a person only when he is capable of standing open to all the gifts which are prepared for him.

Giving can easily become a means of manipulation where the man who receives the gift becomes dependent on the will of the one who gives it.

When you give, you are the master of the situation, you can dole out the goods to those you think deserving. You have control over the surroundings and you can enjoy the power your possessions give you.

Acceptance is something else. When someone accepts a gift, he admits another into his world and is ready to give him a place in his own being. If someone gives a painting to his friend, he asks his friend to give it a place in his own home. Ultimately, a gift becomes a gift only when it is accepted. When the gift is accepted, it acquires a place in the life of the other. It is also understandable that many people want to give a gift in return as soon as possible, thereby reestablishing the balance and getting rid of any dependence relationship. Between people, it is quite often more a question of trading than accepting, and many people are even embarrassed with a present because they know of no way they can reciprocate. "It makes me feel obligated," they say.

Perhaps the challenge of the gospel lies precisely in the invitation to accept a gift for which we can give nothing in return. For the gift is the life breath of God himself, the Spirit who is poured out on us through Jesus Christ. This life breath frees us from fear and gives us new room to live. A man who prayerfully goes about his life is constantly ready to receive the breath of God, and to let his life be renewed and expanded. The man who never prays, on the contrary, is like the child with asthma; because he is short of breath, the whole world shrivels up before him. He creeps in a corner gasping for air, and is virtually in agony. But the man who prays opens himself to God and can freely breathe again. He stands upright, stretches out his hands and comes out of his corner, free to boldly stride through the world because he can move about without fear.

A man who prays is one who can once more breathe freely, who has the freedom to move where he wishes with no fears to haunt him.

The man who lives from God's breath can recognize with joy that the same breath sinks into the lungs of his fellowman, and that they are both drawing from the same source. At this mutual realization, the fear of another disappears, a smile comes to the lips, the weapons fall, and one hand reaches out for the other. He who recognizes the breath of God in another can truly let another enter his life, too, and can receive the gifts which are given to him. In this way it is possible to allow another the joy of giving something.

The difficulty this presents in our time comes out in this confession of a contemporary man: "To accept something gives me the feeling of dependence. This is something I'm generally not used to. I manage my own affairs and I'm glad I can. Whenever I receive something, I don't know exactly how to handle it. It's as though I am no longer the center of my own life and it gets a little uncomfortable. Actually that's a silly thing to say, for I'm not letting someone else have what I myself like to have. I don't let him have the joy of giving."

But when you notice that someone accepts you, you want to give everything in return and you discover that you have much more to give than you thought.

Then you too can sing with Simon and Garfunkel:

Here is my song for the asking
Ask me and I will play
So sweetly, I'll make you smile
This is my tune for the taking
Take it, don't turn away
I've been waiting all my life
Ask me and I will play
All the love that I hold inside.

In this prayerful acceptance for each other, there is no place left for prejudice, for instead of defining another, I always let him appear to me as ever new. Then people can talk to one another and share their lives in a way where heart speaks to heart. One student writes: "A good conversation is a process where we give each other life and meaning to go on, to celebrate together, to be sad together and to inspire one another."

Above all, praying means to be accepting toward God who is always new, always different. For God is a deeply moved God whose heart is greater than mine. The open acceptance of prayer in the face of an ever-new God makes me free. In prayer, I am constantly on the way, on pilgrimage. On my way, I meet more and more people who show me something about him whom I seek. I'll never know if I've reached him. But I do know that he will always be new and there is no reason for fear.

A man who prays is a man who has the courage to stretch out his arms and to let himself be led. After Jesus had given Peter the commission to care for his people, he said:

I tell you most solemnly,
when you were young
you put on your own belt
and walked where you liked;
but when you grow old
you will stretch out your hands,
and somebody else will put a belt around you
and take you where you would rather not go.
(John 21:18)

Care for your fellowman means a growing acceptance. This acceptance led Jesus and his disciples to where they didn't want to go, to the cross. That is also the road for the man who prays. When you are still young and not yet adult, you want to hold everything in your own hands, but if you have your hands open toward prayer, you are able to stretch out your arms and let yourself be led without knowing where. You know only that the freedom which God's breath has brought you will lead to new life, even if the cross is the only sign of it you can see.

But for the man who prays, even that sign has lost its fearful character.

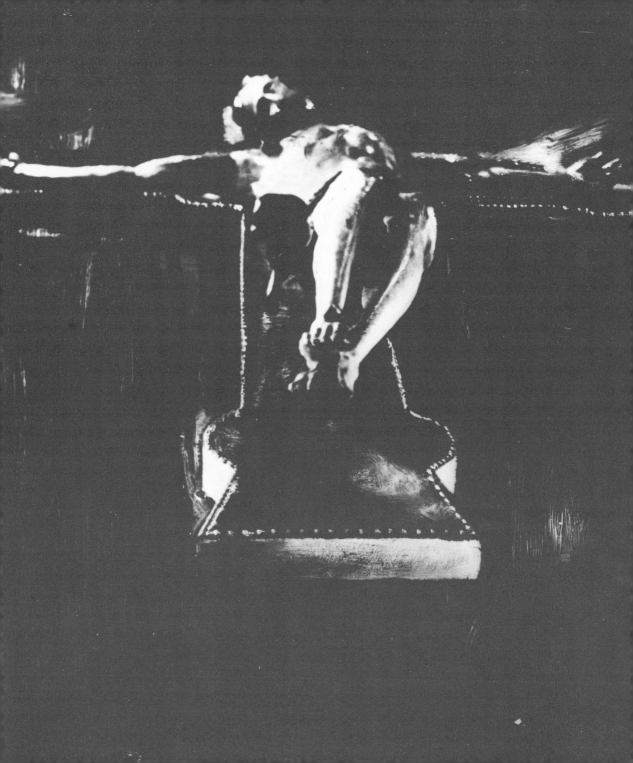

CHAPTER 3

Prayer and Hope

IN the silence of prayer you can spread out your hands to embrace nature, God, and your fellowman. This acceptance not only means that you are ready to look at your own limitations, but that you expect the coming of something new. For this reason, every prayer is an expression of hope. A man who expects nothing from the future cannot pray. He says in the words of Bertold Brecht:

> As it is, it will stay
> What we want will never come.

For this man, life stands still. Spiritually, he is dead. There can be life and there can be movement only when you no longer accept things as they are now, and you look ahead toward that which is not yet.

And yet, if you think about prayer, it seems that we always do something more like asking than hoping. And it can hardly be otherwise. Most of the time, we speak of prayer only when specific momentary circumstances give rise to it. When there is war, we pray for peace, when there is drought, we pray for rain, when we go on vacation, we pray for nice weather, when a test is coming, we pray that we'll pass, when a friend is sick, we pray that he'll get well, and when someone dies, we pray for his eternal rest. Our prayer is in the midst of our lives and is interwoven with everything else which busies our day. It is also true of prayer that whatever fills the heart is what the mouth pours forth.

And our hearts are filled with many concrete and tangible desires and expectations. Mother hopes her son will come home on time. Father hopes he'll get a promotion. A boy dreams of the girl he loves, and the child thinks of the bicycle he was promised. Often our thoughts are no further than a couple of hours ahead of us, a couple of days, a couple of weeks, and only seldom a couple of years. We can hardly let ourselves think too far in advance, for the world we live in requires us to focus our attention on the here and now. If we pray, and really pray, we can hardly escape the fact that our cares for the moment, big and small, will fill our prayer and often make it nothing but a long list of requests.

Often this prayer of petition is treated with a certain disdain. Sometimes we regard it as less than prayer of thanksgiving and certainly less than prayer of praise. Prayer of petition is supposedly more egocentric because the person is putting his own interests first and trying to get something for himself. The prayer of thanksgiving, it is said, is directed more toward God, even if it is in connection with gifts which he has given us. And prayer of praise is devoted directly to God for his own sake apart from anything we may or may not have received from him.

But the question is whether this distinction helps us understand what prayer is. The important thing about prayer is not whether it is classified as petition, thanksgiving or praise, but whether it is a prayer of hope or of little faith.

The prayer of little faith is where you hold fast to the concrete of the present situation in order to win a certain security. The prayer of little faith is filled with wishes which beg for immediate fulfillment. This prayer of wish fulfillment has a Santa Claus naivete which wants to satisfy specific desires. When the prayer is not heard, that is, when you don't get the present you wanted, there is disappointment, even hard feelings and bitterness.

It is understandable, therefore, that this prayer of little faith has a great deal of fear and anxiety about it. If you pray like the man of little faith for health, success, an advancement, for peace or whatever else, then you get so set on the concrete request that you feel left in the cold when the expected present doesn't arrive. You even say to yourself: "See what I told you, it doesn't work anyway." With this prayer of little faith, it is the concreteness of the wishes which eliminates the possibility for hope. In this prayer, you want to be certain about what is uncertain and you start thinking in terms of one bird in the hand is better than two or ten birds still in the bush. With this prayer, the petition is aimed at getting what you ask for, any way you can, instead of being directed toward the person who might or might not be able to make that wish come true. The man of little faith prays like a child who wants a present from Santa Claus, but who becomes frightened and runs away as soon as he gets his hands on the package. He would rather have nothing more to do with the old bearded gentleman. All the attention is on the gift and none on the one who gives it. It's as though you were putting on blinders, and your spiritual life is reduced to a beeline toward what you want.

Because he is so eager to arrange for his own future, the man of little faith closes himself off from what, in fact, might be coming. He has no patience with the unspecified promise and he has no trust in the unseen situations which the future has in store. Therefore, when the man of little faith prays, it is a prayer without hope. Likewise, it is without despair, for despair is only possible for someone who knows what it means to hope.

The man of little faith prays a prayer that is carefully reckoned, even stingy, and which is upset by every risk. There is no danger of despair and no chance for hope. The man becomes a midget in a world of tiny things.

The immense difference between hope and wishes comes out in the remarks of a student who wrote: "I see hope as an attitude where everything stays open before me. Not that I don't think of my future in those moments, but I think of it in an entirely different way. Daring to stay open to whatever today will offer me, or tomorrow, two months from now or a year from now, that is hope. To go fearlessly into things without knowing how they'll turn out, to keep on going, even when something doesn't work the first time, to have trust in whatever you're doing."

A man with hope does not get tangled up with concerns for how his wishes will be fulfilled. So, too, his prayer is not directed toward the gift, but toward the one who gives it. His prayer might still contain just as many desires, but ultimately it is not a question of having a wish come true but of expressing an unlimited faith in the giver of all good things. You wish that . . . but you hope for. . . . For the prayer of hope, it is essential that there are no guarantees asked, no conditions posed, and no proofs demanded, only that you expect everything from the other without binding him in any way. Hope is based on the premise that the other gives only what is good. Hope includes an openness by which you wait for the other to make his loving promise come true, even though you never know when, where or how this might happen.

Perhaps, in the long run, there is no finer image for the prayer of hope than the relation of a child toward his mother. All day long the child asks for things, but the love he has for his mother does not depend on her fulfilling these wishes. The child knows that his mother will do only what is good for him and in spite of occasional fits and a few short-lived tantrums, if he doesn't get his way, he continues to be convinced that, in the end, his mother does only what she knows is best for him.

The man who prays with hope might still ask for many things, he might ask for everything, and very concretely, like nice weather or an advancement. This concreteness is even a sign of authenticity. For if you ask only for faith, hope, love, freedom, happiness, modesty, humility, etc., without making them concrete in the nitty-gritty of daily life, you probably haven't really involved God in your real life. But if you pray in hope, all those concrete requests are merely ways of expressing your unlimited trust in him who fulfills all his promises, who holds out for you nothing but good, and who wants for himself nothing more than to share his goodness with you.

Only if you pray with hope can you break through the barriers of death. For no longer do you want to know what it will be like after you die, what heaven exactly will mean, how you will be eternal, or how the risen Lord will show himself. You don't let yourself be distracted by daydreams where all your conflicting desires are satisfied in a wish-come-true hereafter. When you pray with hope, you turn yourself toward a God who will bring forth his promises; it is enough to know that he is a faithful God.

This hope gives you a new freedom which lets you look realistically at life without feeling dejected. This freedom comes through in the words of the man who wrote:

Hope means to keep living
amid desperation
and to keep humming
in the darkness.
Hoping is knowing that there is love,
it is trust in tomorrow
it is falling asleep
and waking again
when the sun rises.
In the midst of a gale at sea,
it is to discover land.
In the eyes of another
It is to see that he understands you.
. . . .
As long as there is still hope
There will also be prayer.
. . . .
And God will be holding you
in his hands.

In this way, every prayer of petition becomes a prayer of thanksgiving and praise as well, precisely because it is a prayer of hope. In the hopeful prayer of petition, we thank God for his promise and we praise him for his trust.

Our numerous requests simply become the concrete way of saying that we trust in the fullness of God's goodness, which he wants to share with us. Whenever we pray with hope, we put our lives in the hands of God. Fear and anxiety fade away and everything we are given and everything we are deprived of is nothing but a finger pointing out the direction of God's hidden promise which we shall taste in full.

CHAPTER 4

Prayer and Compassion

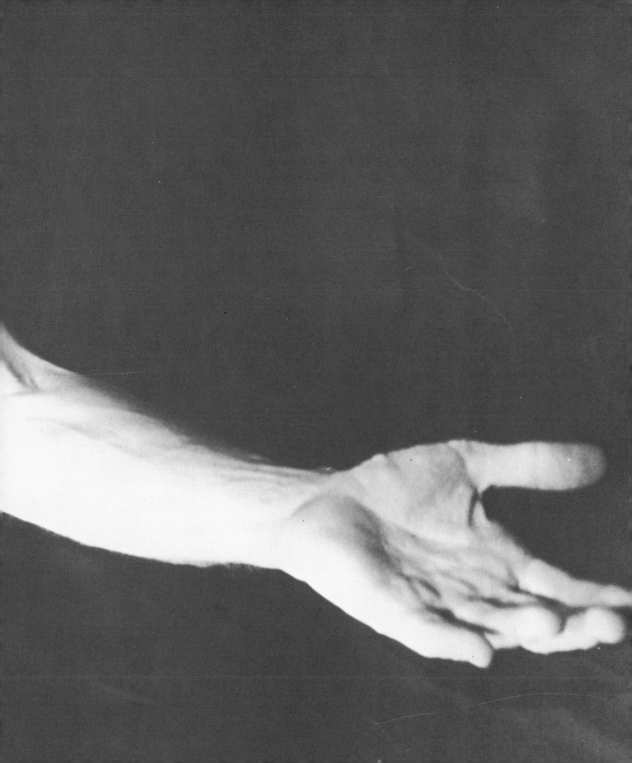

IF you are to have a future, it will be a future together with others. A prayer of hope is a prayer that disarms you and extends you far beyond the limits of your own longings. Therefore, there can be no talk of prayer so long as praying is thought of as an activity which excludes our fellowman. "Anyone who says, 'I love God,' and hates his brother is a liar," says St. John (I Jn 4:20). And Jesus says: "It is not those who say to me, 'Lord, Lord,' who will enter the kingdom of heaven, but the person who does the will of my Father in heaven" (Matt 7:21).

Praying can never be antisocial or asocial. Whenever you pray and leave out your fellowman, your prayer is no longer real prayer. But that is not as clear-cut as it sounds. There are many who say: "Go out and do something for your fellowman instead of praying for him." Now, it would be exaggerating to suppose that the reason so little is getting done is because people spend so much time praying for one another. But it is clear that not seldom prayer is written off as fruitless and the comment, "I'll pray for you," is more often seen as a meaningless remark than as a sign of genuine concern.

In the thinking of modern, active, energetic man, praying and living have come to be so widely separated that bringing them together seems almost impossible. But here lies the central problem: How can your prayer be truly necessary for the welfare of your fellowman? How could it be that you should "pray always" and that prayer is the "one thing necessary"? The question becomes important only when it is posed in its most exacting form. The question of when or how to pray is not really the most important one. The crucial question is whether you should pray always and whether your prayer is necessary. Here, the stakes are all or nothing! If someone says that it's good to turn to God in prayer for a spare minute, or if he grants that a person with a problem does well to take refuge in prayer, he has as much as admitted that praying is on the margin of life and that it doesn't really matter.

Whenever you feel that a little praying can't do any harm, you will find that it can't do much good either. Prayer has meaning only if it is necessary and indispensable. Prayer is prayer only when we can say that without it, a man could not live. How can this be true, or be made true? The word that brings us closest to an answer to this question is the word "compassion." To understand this, you must first examine what happens to a man when he prays. Then you can comprehend how you can meet your fellowman in prayer.

The man who looks prayerfully on the world is the man who does not expect happiness from himself, but who looks forward toward the other who is coming. It is often said that a man who prays is conscious of his dependence, and in his prayer he expresses his helplessness. This can easily be misunderstood. The praying man not only says, "I can't do it and I don't understand it," but also, "Of myself, I don't have to be able to do it, and of myself, I don't have to understand it." When you stop at that first phrase, you often pray in confusion and despair, but when you can also add the second, you feel your dependence no longer as helplessness but as a happy openness which looks forward to being renewed.

If you view your weakness as a disgrace, you will come to rely on prayer only in extreme need and you will come to consider prayer as a forced confession of your impotence. But if you see your weakness as that which makes you worth loving, and if you are always prepared to be surprised at the power the other gives you, you will discover through praying that living means living together.

A prayer which makes you lose heart can hardly be called a prayer. For you lose heart only when you still presume that you must be able to do everything, that every gift to you from the other is a proof of inferiority, and that you are a full man only when you no longer have any need of the other.

Every time a despondent man undergoes the painful discovery that he has failed, he is ashamed and hangs his head. Finally, he becomes weary and exhausted from the tension of the effort to prove that he can do it alone. He loses the buoyancy of life and becomes bitter. He concludes that his fellowmen are enemies and rivals who have outwitted him. This tension condemns him to loneliness because every hand which reaches out for him is seen as a threat to his sense of honor.

If you address yourself in prayer to God who is completely the other, you are searching for true peace in your life. When God asked Adam, the man, "Where are you?" Adam answered, "I was hiding" (Gen 3:9-10) and here he was confessing his true condition. But this confession set him on his way to God. The praying man is he who comes out of his shelter and not only has the courage to see his own poverty but also sees that there is no enemy to hide from, only a friend who would like nothing better than to clothe him with his own coat.

Certainly praying takes some admissions, that is, recognition of your state as a man. But this admission does not lead to shame, to a feeling of worthlessness or despair, but rather to the discovery that you are a man and God is God. If you cling tightly to your own weakness, your faults, shortcomings and your twisted past, to all the events, facts and situations which you would prefer to cut out of your own history, you're only hiding behind a hedge which everyone can see through. What you've done is narrowed your world to a small hiding place, where you try to conceal yourself, suspecting rather pitifully that everyone has been seeing you all along.

Praying means giving up a false security, no longer looking for arguments which will protect you if you get pushed into a corner, no longer setting your hope on a couple of lighter moments which your life might still offer. Praying means to stop expecting from God that same small-mindedness which you discover in yourself. To pray is to walk in the full light of God, and to say simply, without holding back, "I am a man and you are God." At that moment, conversion occurs, the restoration of the true relationship. Man is not the one who once in a while makes a mistake and God is not the one who now and then forgives. No, man is a sinner and God is love. Conversion makes this obvious with a stunning simplicity and a disarming clarity.

This conversion brings with it the relaxation which lets you breathe again and puts you at rest in the embrace of a forgiving God. The experience results in a calm and simple joy. For then you can say: "I don't know the answer and I can't do this thing, but I don't have to know it, and I don't have to be able to do it." This new knowledge is the liberation which gives you access to everything in creation and leaves you free to play in the garden which lays before you.

The man who prays not only discovers himself and God, but in the same meeting he discovers who his neighbor is. For in prayer, you not only profess that man is man and God is God, but also, that your neighbor is your fellowman, that is, a man alongside you. For if your conversion has brought you down to the bottom of your human nature, you notice that you are not alone: Being a man means being together.

At precisely this point, compassion is born. This compassion is not covered by the word "pity," nor by the word "sympathy." Pity has the connotation of too much distance. Sympathy gives the impression of an exclusive nearness. Compassion has nothing of distance and nothing of exclusiveness about it.

Compassion includes various moments. In the first place, it shows you that your neighbor is a man who shares his humanity with you. This partnership cuts through all walls which might have kept you separate. Across all barriers of land and language, wealth and poverty, knowledge and ignorance, we are still one, created from the same dust, subject to the same laws and destined for the same end. With this compassion you can say, "In the expression of the oppressed I recognize my own face and in the hands of the oppressed, I recognize my own hands which speak of powerlessness and helplessness. His flesh is my flesh, his blood is my blood, his pain is my pain and his smile is my smile. There is nothing in me that he would find strange, and there is nothing in him that I would not recognize. In my heart, I know his yearning for love, and down to my entrails I can feel his cruelty. In his eyes, I see my plea for forgiveness and in his hardened frown, I see my refusal. When he murders, I know that I too could have done that, and when he gives birth, I know that I am capable of that as well. In the depths of my being, I have met my fellowman for whom nothing is strange, neither love nor hate, nor life, nor death."

Compassion is daring to acknowledge our mutual destiny so that we might move forward all together into the land which God is showing us. Compassion also means sharing another's joy which can be just as difficult as suffering with him. To give another the chance to be completely happy and to let his joy blossom to the full. Often you can do nothing more than present a bleached smile and say with some effort, "That's really good for you," or "I'm glad to see you made it."

But this compassion is more than a shared slavery with the same fear and same sighs of relief, and more than a shared joy. For if your compassion is born of prayer, it is born of your meeting with God who is also the God of your fellowman. At the moment when you grant that God is God who wants to be your God, and when you give him access to yourself, you realize that a new way has been opened for the man who is beside you. He too has no reason to fear, he too does not have to hide behind a hedge, he too needs no weapons to be a man. The garden which has been unattended for so long is also meant for him.

Conversion to God, therefore, means a simultaneous conversion to the other persons who live with you on this earth. The farmer, the worker, the student, the prisoner, the sick, the black man, the white man, the weak, the strong, the oppressed and the oppressor, the patient and the one who heals, the tortured and the torturer, the boss and the flunky, not only are they people like you, but they are also called to make themselves heard and to give God a chance to be the God of all.

Thus compassion removes all pretensions, just as it removes false modesty. It invites you to understand everything, to see yourself in the light of God and to joyfully tell everyone you meet that there is no reason to fear; the land is free to be cultivated and to yield a rich harvest.

It is not so simple, however. Risks are involved. For compassion means to lay a bridge over to the other without knowing whether he wants to be reached. Your fellowman might be so embittered that he doesn't expect anything from you. Then your compassion stirs up enmity and it is difficult not to become sour yourself and say, "You see what I told you, it doesn't work anyhow." And yet, compassion is possible when it has roots in prayer. For in prayer you are not based on your own strength, not on the good will of another, but only on trust in God. That is why prayer is primarily a calling to find your own place in this world and to live in that place. There it is that you not only discover that you exist, but you meet people next to you, who with you will cultivate and develop the new world.

CHAPTER 5

Prayer and Revolution

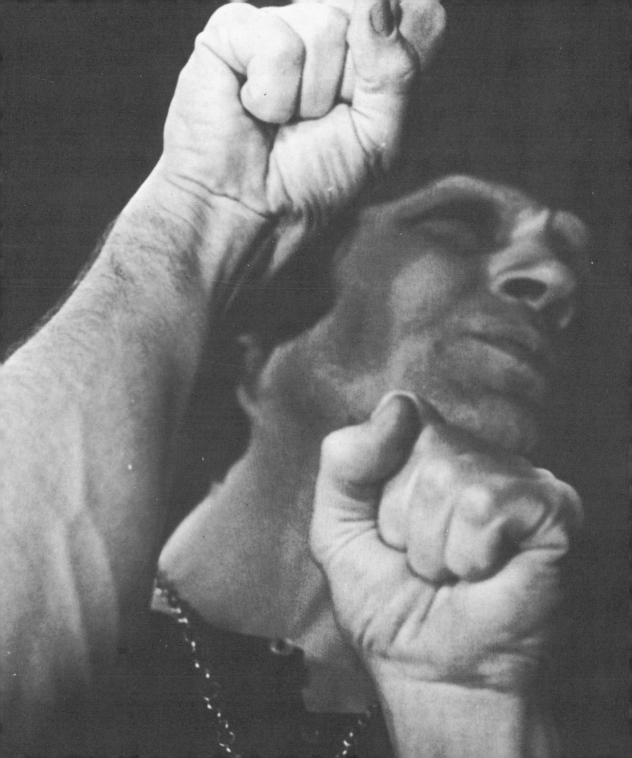

WHEN your life is more and more becoming a prayer, you notice that you are always busy converting yourself and gaining an ever-deeper understanding of your fellowman. You notice, too, that prayer is the pulse of the world you live in. If you are really praying, you can't help but have critical questions about the great problems the world is grappling with, and you can't get rid of the idea that a conversion is not only necessary for yourself and your neighbor, but for the entire human community. This conversion of the world means a "turning-around," a revolution, which can lead to renewal.

At first glance, the words "prayer" and "revolution" seem to be at such opposite extremes and to come from such different worlds that their combination probably invokes only resentment and irritation. This irritation is a good place to begin, for in our day, the irritated man seems to ask for more attention than the man who prays.

The irritation and resentment which get so many people up in arms, which confuse them and prompt them to protest and demonstrate — or, in defiance, to do nothing or to flee to a drugged oblivion — these are unmistakable signs of a deeply rooted dissatisfaction with the world where we are forced to live out our lives. Some would like to remind our society of those ideals of freedom and justice which are written in the books but which are trampled underfoot in everyday practice. Some have even given up this effort and have come to the conclusion that the only chance left for a man to find peace and calm is to retreat from this chaotic world. They turn in disgust from society with its institutions and plans. Whatever one does, whether he becomes a hippie, a yippie, a revolutionary or a meek dreamer, whether one calls for the changing of structures or lets it all float by with a melancholy grin, the resentment remains, fierce and discernible or deeply suppressed beneath an attitude of passive indifference. It is not hard to distinguish in all these phenomena a deep longing for another world. The society as it is now must change, its false structures must disappear and something entirely new must take their place. One man goes into the struggle with all the energy he can muster, another waits for it as for an apparition which he cannot bring about himself, a third anticipates the future and melts into a forced dreamworld of sound, color and form in which, at least for the moment, he can pretend that everything, even himself, has been made new.

What is perhaps most striking about the visions of the world's future is that they have taken form completely independent of Christian thinking which is preeminently future-orientated. Those enormous powers which are gaining ground in the hardened world, which cry out for a new age, a new world, and a new order can find no solid roots in traditional Christianity, it seems. While Christians were busy with their interior household problems and were so preoccupied with themselves that they lost sight of the rest of the world, a growing need for salvation outside of Christianity became more and more evident. This suggestion Christians often regarded as merely naive, anarchical and immature.

And yet you are Christian only so long as you look forward to a new world, so long as you constantly pose critical questions to the society you live in, so long as you emphasize the need of conversion both for yourself and for the world, so long as you in no way let yourself become established in a situation of seeming calm, so long as you stay unsatisfied with the status quo and keep saying that a new world is yet to come. You are Christian only when you believe that you have a role to play in the realization of this new kingdom, and when you urge everyone you meet with a holy unrest to make haste so that the promise might soon be fulfilled. So long as you live as a Christian you keep looking for a new order, a new structure, a new life.

You can't bear it that someone stands still along the way, loses heart and seeks his happiness in little pleasures which he can cling to. It irritates you to see things established and settled and you resent all that self-indulgence and self-satisfaction, for you know with an indestructible certainty that something greater is coming, and you've already seen the first rays of light. As a Christian, you not only maintain that this world will pass, but that it has to pass to allow a new world to be born, and that there will never be a moment in this life when you can rest assured that there is nothing more to do.

But are there any Christians? If we get the impression that Christianity today is failing in its role of spiritual leadership, if it appears that men who seek for the meaning of being and non-being, of birth and death, of loving and being loved, of being young and growing old, of giving and receiving, of hurting and being hurt expect no response from the witnesses to Jesus Christ, you begin to wonder to just what degree these witnesses should be calling themselves Christians.

The Christian witness is a revolutionary witness because the Christian professes that the Lord will come again and make all things new. The Christian life is a revolutionary life because the Christian assumes a critical distance from the world and in spite of all contradictions, he keeps saying that a new man and a new peace are possible and they cannot come about without us.

Therefore, it is not so much a question of making a Christian into a revolutionary as of being willing to recognize in the contemporary revolutionary the authentic features of Christ. For maybe in this man who makes no peace with his world, and who gives himself wholly over to the struggle for a better future, we can once more find him who gave his life for the freedom of many.

What are these features which mark a true revolutionary? Whenever we look for them, we must understand that these features will never be perfectly evident in any individual person. It is always a question of reactions, fingerprints, references, footprints or notches on a tree which makes us suspect that someone has passed by who is worth investigating.

Who is this man? He is a person who has a great deal of attracting power for those around him. Those who meet him are fascinated by him and want to know more about him. All he comes in contact with get the irresistible impression that he derives his strength from a hidden source which is strong and rich. An inner freedom flows out from him, giving him an independence which is neither haughty nor aloof, but which enables him to stand above immediate needs and most pressing necessities. He is moved by what happens around him, but he doesn't let it oppress or shatter him. He listens attentively, speaks with a self-possessed authority, but doesn't easily get rushed or excited. In everything he says and does, he seems to have a lively vision before him which those who hear him can intimate, but cannot see. This vision leads his life. He is obedient to it. Through it he knows how to distinguish between what is important and what is not. Many things which seem of gripping immediacy hardly stir him, and he attaches great importance to some things which others simply let pass.

He is not insensitive to what moves other men, but he gives their needs another meaning by holding them up against his own vision. He is happy and glad to have people listen to him, but he is not out to form groups around himself, to build up an organization or to launch a movement. No cliques can grow up around him for he attaches himself exclusively to no one. What he says and does has a convincing ring and even a self-evident truth, but he forces his opinions on no one and is not annoyed when someone doesn't adopt his opinion or doesn't do as he wishes.

In everything, he seems to have a concrete and living goal in mind, the realization of which is of vital importance. Yet he himself maintains a great inner freedom in the light of this goal. Often it seems as though he knows that he will never see the goal achieved, and that he only sees the shadow of it himself. But, throughout, he has an impressive freedom from the course of his own life. He is careful and cautious, certainly not reckless, and yet it comes out at every turn that he counts his life as of secondary importance. He doesn't live merely to hold out but to work out a new world, the outlines of which he sees and which make such a call to him that the barriers between his life and his death have become blurred.

But it is also plain that a revolutionary man not only draws men to him, he repels them as well. The offense he provokes is just as great a reality as the attractiveness he displays. Precisely because he is so free from things which many men hold sacred, he is a threat to them. His manner of speaking and living constantly relativizes the values which many men have built their lives upon. They feel the penetrating depth of his message and see the consequences for themselves if they should grant that he is right. Again and again when he is among them, they know that the world he lives in is also the world they are longing for, but it demands too much of them to actually let them strive toward it. His criticism of their lives is so insistent and unmasking that the only way for them to escape it is to get rid of him. In order to uphold their tranquility of mind and to no longer be disturbed in their secure way of life, they find it necessary to silence the one who fights against their phony and artificial happiness.

A person, therefore, who would proclaim a new world and set the old world reeling becomes the occasion for a stifling aggression at the hands of those very ones who consider themselves the protectors of the order and the upholders of peace and calm. Above all, for those who provide the leadership in the present-day world, this man unmasks the illusion of the age and is an intolerable agitator of restlessness. From their point of view they are right, for this visionary not only has criticism for the leaders but for the societies they are guiding. The aggression stirred up against the visionary usually results in his excommunication with all the means the prevailing order has at its disposal. This can start with a denial of his message, expand to verbal attacks, and end with imprisonment and even execution. But if the revolutionary was credible and true, what is expected never happens. Not even his death disturbs his calling. Those who killed him will often discover to their surprise and horror that they have, in fact, only succeeded in awakening many more and that the cry for a new world has grown still louder.

From this description, no person in our world could be classified as a revolutionary. Any name we might mention could offer only small traces of this man. And yet it must be said that anyone who opens his eyes and looks for this man can find him among the thousands whom he meets in his lifetime. Sometimes only vaguely recognizable, sometimes undeniably evident, never totally, but the parts becoming ever plainer for those who want to see. We can see him in the guerilla fighter, in the youth with the demonstration sign, in the quiet dreamer in the corner of a cafe, in the soft-spoken monk, in the meek student, in the mother who lets her son go his own way, in the father who reads to his child from a strange book, in the smile of a girl, in the indignation of a worker, in every man who in one way or another draws his power to live from a vision which he sees looming before him, which surpasses everything else he has ever heard or seen.

What does this have to do with prayer? Praying means breaking through the veil of existence and allowing yourself to be led by the vision which has become real to you. Whatever we call that vision: "the Unseen Reality," "the total Other," "the Numen," "the Spirit," "the Father," we repeatedly assert that it is not man himself who possesses the power to make the revolution, the "turning around" come to pass. It is rather the power which has revealed itself to him and with which he feels he is eternally united.

The praying man is the man who inspires the world, who looks on it with compassion and, in this glance, penetrates to the source of all being.

Often we use the word God. This word can suggest something fascinating as well as something horrible. It attracts and it repels. It is seductive and dangerous. It can just as well nourish man as swallow him up. It is like the sun. Without the sun, there could be no human life, but if a man comes too close, he is burned. The Christian is a man who knows that It is a Person, and that God's name is Abba, Father. He knows that it is possible to enter into dialogue with him and so work at renewing the earth. Praying, therefore, is the most critical activity man is capable of for a man who prays is never satisfied with the world of here and now, he is constantly striving to realize the new world, the first rays of which he has already seen.

When you pray, you open yourself to the influence of the Power which has revealed itself as Love. The Power gives you freedom and independence. Once touched by this Power, you are no longer swayed back and forth by the countless opinions, ideas and feelings which flow through you. You have found a center for your life that gives you a creative distance so that everything you see, hear and feel can be tested against the source. Christ is the man who in the most revealing way made clear that prayer means sharing in the power of God. It enabled him to turn his world around, it gave him the attraction to draw countless men out of the chains of their existence, but it also stirred up aggression which brought him to his death. Christ, who is called the Son of Man and also the Son of God, has shown what it means to pray. In him, God himself became visible for the fall and rise of many.

Prayer is a revolutionary matter because once you begin, you put your entire life in the balance. If you really set about praying, that is, truly enter into the reality of the unseen, you must realize that you are daring to express a most fundamental criticism, a criticism which many are waiting for, but which will be too much for many others.

Praying, therefore, means being constantly ready to let go of your certainty and to move on further than where you now are. It demands that you take to the road again and again, leaving your house and looking forward to a new land for yourself and your fellowman. This is why praying demands poverty, that is, the readiness to live a life in which you have nothing to lose so that you always begin afresh. Whenever you willingly choose this poverty you make yourself vulnerable, but you also become free to see the world and to let the world be seen in its true form. For you have no need to defend yourself and you can tell loudly what you know through your intimate contact with him who is the source of all life. But this demands courage. If you are to make real all the consequences of a prayerful life, you might well be frightened and wonder if you should dare. Then it is vital to remember that courage is also a gift from God for which you can pray with words like these:

God give me the courage to be revolutionary
As your Son Jesus Christ was.
Give me the courage to loosen myself from this world.
Teach me to stand up free
and to shun no criticism.
God, it is for your kingdom.
Make me free,
make me poor in this world,
Then will I be rich in the real world,
which this life is all about.
God, thank you for the vision of the future,
but make it fact and not just theory.

CONCLUSION

With Open Hands

To pray means to open your hands before God. It means slowly relaxing the tension which squeezes your hands together and accepting your existence with an increasing readiness, not as a possession to defend, but as a gift to receive. Above all, therefore, prayer is a way of life which allows you to find a stillness in the midst of the world where you open your hands to God's promises, and find hope for yourself, your fellowman and the whole community in which you live. In prayer, you encounter God in the soft breeze, in the distress and joy of your neighbor and in the loneliness of your own heart.

Prayer leads you to see new paths and to hear new melodies in the air. Prayer is the breath of your life which gives you freedom to go and stay where you wish and to find the many signs which point out the way to a new land. Praying is not simply some necessary compartment in the daily schedule of a Christian or a source of support in time of need, nor is it restricted to Sunday morning or as a frame to surround mealtimes. Praying is living. A Benedictine monk living in India writes:

There are no part-time contemplatives, just as there are no part-time Christians, nor part-time men. From the day that we begin to believe in Christ and acknowledge him as Lord, there is no moment — awake, asleep, walking, sitting, working, learning, eating, playing that is not marked by God's hold on us, which is not lived in the name of Jesus in the inspiration of the Holy Spirit.

(PRAYER by Abhishiktenanda, Delhi. 1967)

Therefore, a life in prayer is a life with open hands where you are not ashamed of your weakness but realize that it is more perfect for a man to be led by the other than to seek to hold everything in his own hands.

Only within this kind of life does a spoken prayer make sense. A prayer in church, at table or in school is only a witness to what we want to make of our entire lives. Such a prayer only recalls to mind that praying is living and it invites you to make this an ever-greater reality. Thus there are as many ways to pray as there are moments in life. Sometimes you seek out a quiet spot and you want to be alone, sometimes you look for a friend and you want to be together. Sometimes you'd like a book or some music. Sometimes you want to sing out with hundreds, sometimes only to whisper with a few. Sometimes you want to say it with words, sometimes with a deep silence.

In all these moments, you gradually make your life more a prayer and you open your hands to be led by God even to where you would rather not go.